THE LI
BOOK OF
RUDE
WORDS

Sid Finch

summersdale

THE LITTLE BOOK OF RUDE WORDS

First published in 2009 as *Really Rude Words*
Reprinted in 2011
This revised and updated edition copyright © Summersdale Publishers Ltd, 2016

Research by Stewart Ferris and Anna Martin

Summersdale Publishers Ltd
46 West Street
Chichester
West Sussex
PO19 1RP
UK

www.summersdale.com

Printed and bound in the Malta

ISBN: 978-1-84953-845-9

Substantial discounts on bulk quantities of Summersdale books are available to corporations, professional associations and other organisations. For details contact Nicky Douglas by telephone: +44 (0) 1243 756902, fax: +44 (0) 1243 786300 or email: nicky@summersdale.com.

CONTENTS

INTRODUCTION

We all know the F-word and the C-word, but it's time to get inventive. Within the sweaty confines of this dirty little book you will find an inspirational and, dare we say it, educational collection of offensive terms with examples of how you can integrate such gems as *arse fuck*, *clunge* and *schlong* into everyday discourse.

From the rude and the crude to the downright filthy, there's nothing quite like throwing in a well-placed profanity to raise the conversational bar. Whether you're slightly hacked off with your partner ('You're such a flange!') or you're driving the point home in an important board meeting ('Time to blue ball the big man!'), everybody is doing it, so don't be a dickwad – get on the bandwagon!

RUDE WORDS: AN A-Z

ARSE

Definition:

An area of the body which is sat on, shat through and groped during slow dances, often all in the same evening.

....

Usage:

'Arse!' – generally applicable at times of disappointment, such as when your new lover expresses a keen interest in celibacy.

'My arse!' – someone proudly posting their belfie (bum selfie).

'Does my arse look big in this?' – to which the answer is, 'Yes it does.'

ARSE FUCK

Definition:

To fuck someone up the arse; in reference to someone so minging that you would rather be shafted up the rear than look at their hideous gnome-like phizog.

....

Usage:

'Get behind me, arse fuck' – your hideous form is making my corneas burn, so please kindly move to the back of the bus.

'You don't have to be such an arse fuck' – you don't have to be ugly; plastic surgery is quite cheap these days so get yourself a face transplant.

'That was a complete arse fuck' – you gave me a very thorough rogering up my back passage, for which I thank you.

Definition:

A slightly more parent-friendly version of arse fuck; to make a hash of something; a bottom excretion, i.e. poo.

....

Usage:

'It's arse fudge!' – you've done a shoddy job.

'It's arse fudge!' – I do believe that you've just shat your pants *points to brown stain on clothing*

'Arse fudge for all the family!' – one of Willy Wonka's less popular confectionery lines.

ARSEHOLE

Definition:

Someone who demonstrates mental deficiency by pulling out in front of you in their car, spilling your drink in the pub or talking loudly on their phone.

....

Usage:

'You're a complete arsehole' – useful phrase for a plastic surgeon upon completion of anal reconstructive surgery.

'Don't be an arsehole all your life' – try voting for a different party once in a while.

'This place is the arsehole of the earth' – useful phrase if you're in [insert place of choice here].

"Balls"

Definition:

Those of which Hitler had only one; squidgy things that tennis players hit during romp sessions.

....

Usage:

'New balls, please' – Wimbledon umpire after prolonged sex.

'Suck my balls' – a suggestion to someone who is dentally challenged when presented with a plate of meatballs.

'What a load of balls' – remark made by a visitor to a tennis-ball factory.

BEAVER

Definition:

Moist, furry mammal found in damp, dark places; to work very hard with the intention of gaining access to a moist, furry mammal; a woman's genitalia.

....

Usage:

'What a fine beaver' – what a fine moist, furry mammal.

'Can I stroke your beaver?' – be careful that it doesn't bite off your fingers.

'Beaver away' – probably downstream somewhere and working very hard.

BEEF CURTAINS

Definition:

Meaty entrance to a lady's front bottom; hanging device to keep sunlight out of an abattoir.

....

Usage:

'Pull back those beef curtains so I can see if it's damp outside' – phrase used by a butcher at work.

'Pull back those beef curtains so I can see if it's damp inside' – phrase used by a butcher at home.

'Your beef curtains look like a double cheeseburger. Yum' – what you should never say to your lover.

BLUE BALL

Definition:

When a man is very aroused but is unable to relieve himself; a massive build-up of expectation and excitement, but not getting what you want in the end – like Christmas; a blue ball.

....

Usage:

'I had terrible blue ball last night' – what a man would say after trapping his knackers in his flies.

'I don't mean to blue ball you, but...' – I don't mean to leave you hanging, but I need to buy a lottery ticket, so get off me!

'I went to bed with blue balls' – snooker players who take their work home with them.

BOLLOCKS

Definition:

Exclamation made when a potent fart is traced back to you; accusation of lying after you blame your bottom burp on the hamster; a sperm factory kept between a gentleman's legs.

....

Usage:

'Oh, bollocks!' – when you catch your partner smelling your sibling's underwear.

'You're talking a load of bollocks!' – when your partner tries to deny the story in front of the rest of the family.

'Bollocking bollocks that hurt!' – your partner's reaction when you teach them a lesson in morality.

"Boner"

Definition:

When a man has an erection; the bane of all teenage boys in the classroom; an error of judgement; someone who is lazy; a slang term for a trombone.

....

Usage:

'Can I play with your boner?' – may I fiddle with your trombone? I'm a lifelong fan of brass instruments.

'Can I play with your boner?' – a man will always say yes to this question, until he realises you're talking about his trombone.

'That's a massive boner!' – what a cock-up, and I'm not talking about your cock!

CLUNGE

Definition:

Slang for female genitalia; past participle of 'cling' without the 'e'.

....

Usage:

'There's clunge everywhere' – something said by 'proper lads'.

'Can't see the wood for the clunge' – a worthy response when rambling through the trees at a popular dogging spot.

'Clunge ahoy!' – a nautical exclamation by a group of individuals on a stag night.

COCK

Definition:

A male chicken; adjective applicable to any annoying person; a man's ding-dong.

....

Usage:

'You're such a cock' – insult directed at an annoying cockerel.

'Suck my cock' – chat-up line for those who like to try the direct approach.

'Oh, go on, please suck my cock. I washed it last week especially' – backup line for when the direct approach inevitably fails.

"Crap"

Definition:

An old computer; all teams other than the one you support; your chances of getting on in life with this kind of vocabulary; a gambling game played with dice; a plop.

....

Usage:

'Your sexual technique is crap' –
not surprising considering you've only practised on your own.

'I need to take a crap' – don't take it with you unless you're walking the dog, in which case make sure it clears up the mess after you.

'Fancy a crap?' – it's likely you'll do a double take if someone asks you this, but they're actually asking if you would like to partake in an innocent game of dice.

"Dick"

Definition:

A person who drives the wrong way down a one-way street; someone who loudly proclaims unsubstantiated opinions; a trouser-sausage.

....

Usage:

'You're a dick' – if you were going to talk to the parts of your partner's body, this might be a good place to start, except if your partner is female...

'Your opinion means dick all!' – please stop telling me your thoughts about your trouser-sausage.

'Sorry, officer, I'm just a dick' – your excuse for being caught driving the wrong way down a one-way street.

DICKWAD

Definition:

For when you need a slightly stronger insult than 'dick'; a tissue used to mop up jizz.

....

Usage:

'I'm not voting for that dickwad' – I don't believe that person has the credentials or morals to run the country.

'Who's the dickwad, who's the dickwad, who's the dickwad over there' – a drunken chant sung by a bunch of dickwads.

'Are you a dickwad?' – a polite response to a cold-caller asking if you have life insurance.

DILDO

Definition:

A woman's sex stand-in or plastic pal that doesn't go to sleep after one shag; could lead to the eventual extinction of the human race; like tofu, an acceptable meat substitute.

....

Usage:

'I'm having a dildo-rail fitted' – a confused granny talking about wall mouldings (don't correct her, it's funny!).

'Where's my dildo?' – a reliable plan B when your partner has a headache.

'Can I use your dildo?' – to which your answer should always be no, even if they promise to clean it afterwards.

DOUCHE-BAG

Definition:

An obnoxious person with an inflated sense of self-worth – it's a statutory requirement to have one in every workplace; a creep; a phony; something used to clean the nether regions.

....

Usage:

'You utter douchebag' – you should consider applying for that popular business programme next year.

'Has anyone seen my douchebag?' – I could do with a wash and there doesn't seem to be a bidet nearby.

'They're such a douchebag' – the twat at the office party who thinks they're being hilarious by mimicking their colleagues.

FELCH

Definition:

An unfortunately named town; an unfortunate surname; removal by oral means of a gentleman's mayonnaise from the chocolate starfish of another.

....

Usage:

'Taxi driver, please take me to Felch' – make sure you have enough tissues on you.

'Are you felching me or have you just stuck a sardine up my arse?' – to which you reply, 'Just keep your eye on the road, taxi driver.'

'Have you been felching again or is that ice cream on your face?' – it's very hard to tell when it's vanilla flavour.

"Flange"

Definition:

A derogatory word for a lady's love hole, usually implying that the owner of said love hole is undesirable; a projecting rim; the collective noun for baboons; someone who lacks common sense.

....

Usage:

'I really enjoyed that flange last night' – that documentary about baboons was a great piece of television.

'Look at that flange over there!' – when you see someone trying to jump a queue.

'You're such a flange!' – you're a bit of a twat really, aren't you?

FLOATER

Definition:

The really dull person that won't leave you alone, especially at parties; a poo with sufficient gas to float like a brown iceberg that refuses to flush.

....

Usage:

'I couldn't flush the floater' – I've blocked your toilet with a turd that's as fat as a baby's arm.

'I flushed the floater' – I only managed to shake off the weirdo at the party by pushing them in the pool fully clothed.

'I couldn't flush the floater' – a local party candidate describing someone who can't decide which way to vote even when pushed.

FUCK

Definition:

Shag; expression of disappointment when you realise through your drunken stupor that not only has the condom split but your one-night stand is also your cousin.

....

Usage:

'Fancy a fuck?' – a chat-up line with guaranteed results: uncontrollable laughter.

'Fuck! My partner's home early – get into the wardrobe' – make the most of it by searching through pockets for loose change.

'Fuck this for a game of soldiers' – when you've decided to give up hiding in the wardrobe and go home.

"Fuckathon"

Definition:

A prolonged sex session, similar to a marathon except the participants aren't watched by millions of people; an orgy.

....

Usage:

'Looks like there's a fuckathon down at the village hall on Tuesday' – even country types need their kicks.

'Hey, I thought we could go for a fuckathon after lunch on Sunday' – if your friend says this to you, change your phone number.

'I'm participating in a fuckathon – will anyone sponsor me?' – ask your colleagues if they'll chip in!

FUCK KNUCKLE

Definition:

A bit of a wanker; someone who wanks a lot;
could be easily mistaken for a posh character's
name from the popular Jeeves and Wooster books.

....

Usage:

'They're a proper fuck knuckle' – someone hand
that person a family-sized pack of tissues.

'I couldn't give a fuck knuckle' – cats often meow this
when you want them to sit on your lap.

'Oh, fuck knuckle' – what posh people say when
they're caught by their spouse at an insalubrious
Soho-based establishment.

FUCK OFF

Definition:

A request for an annoying twat to go away; an expression of disbelief, such as when you're told it's your turn to wash up.

....

Usage:

'Fuck off!' – I don't want to lose my anal virginity tonight.

'Fuck off!' – please remove yourself from my vicinity forthwith.

'Fuck off!' – what to say to your partner when you're declaring a no-fly zone.

"Green-apple Quickstep"

Definition:

This comes from eating apples when they're not ripe, leading to a bad case of the runs; one of the lesser-known ballroom dances, but it's proved unpopular over the years due to the extensive clean-up job required afterwards.

....

Usage:

'Time to take to the floor for the green-apple quickstep!' – an announcement made before the first dance at a wedding reception after everyone has consumed the warm prawn cocktail.

'I need to do the green-apple quickstep' – I have a pudding in my pants and I believe another helping is on its way.

'It's a TEN for that green-apple quickstep' – rarely heard, except when one of the participants in a ballroom-dancing competition has let their nerves get the better of them.

HOT-DOGGING

Definition:

When a man lays his penis in between another person's bum cheeks, so called because of its similarity in appearance to a hot dog.

....

Usage:

'Do you fancy hotdogging?' – answer with caution if you're not standing near a hot-dog vendor.

'I'm going to be hotdogging tonight!' – if your colleague says this to you, assume they are having a barbecue or you will be having nightmares for weeks.

'I'm going for a hot dog' – I'm going to see if that guy wants to put his penis in between my bum cheeks.

JIZZ

Definition:

Man fluid secreted by the gonads, also known as cum, semen or spunk; the secret ingredient of some fast-food delicacies; helps prevent tooth decay (according to men, anyway).

....

Usage:

'That's so jizz!' – an event that's so epic that it's explosive.

'You're just a jizz junkie!' – when it has become apparent that you haven't wiped your mouth properly.

'I'm going to jizz on you!' – make sure you have your raincoat to hand when someone says this to you.

"Jugs"

Definition:

Receptacles for carrying water or beer; mammalian frontal stereo appendage.

....

Usage:

'Nice jugs. Can I lick them?' – you're entitled to punch anyone who asks you this, unless of course you want them to.

'Nice jugs. Can I photograph them?' – ditto.

'Nice jugs. How much?' – a polite enquiry to a well-endowed homewares assistant.

Definition:

The topiary covering a lady's downstairs parts;
a garden for ladies.

....

Usage:

'Come and play in my lady garden' – come and play
in my garden for ladies, but keep off the grass.

'Does your lady garden need watering?' – a pertinent
question from your gardener during a drought.

'Your lady garden could do with a bit of trimming'
– your genitals are beginning to resemble the
inaccessible parts of the Amazon rainforest;
time to get waxing.

LIMP DICK

Definition:

When a man's mainsail won't rise; a person who lacks credibility; someone who can't play cricket.

....

Usage:

'That was a bit of a limp dick' – very poor show on the cricket field today.

'Have you got a limp dick?' – this is as demoralising for a man to hear as asking him, 'Is it in yet?'

'This company is full of limp dicks' – this company is run by a bunch of idiots who can't get it up, can't play cricket and are morally bankrupt! (Save that one for the Christmas party!)

Definition:

A man who is known for being a bit of a slag, is a legend to his mates and has the local health clinic on speed dial.

Usage:

'He is such a man whore!' – when referring to the guy in your office who is shagging his way through the company.

'Dude, you're such a man whore!' – one man's remark to another, usually accompanied by a congratulatory slap on the back.

'Dude, you're such a man whore!' – do not, under any circumstances, say this in a best man's speech.

Definition:

Someone who feasts from a woman's lady garden with their tongue; a cunning linguist; a carpet licker.

....

Usage:

'I would like a muff diver, please' – a pertinent request when asked by the bartender which cocktail you would like.

'I would like a muff diver, please' – a pertinent request when asked by the bartender what kind of partner you would like.

'I want to be a muff diver when I grow up' – a confused child who thinks hand warmers are farmed in the sea.

"Munter"

Definition:

A person who has fallen out of the ugly tree and has hit all the ugly branches on the way down; an individual of low intelligence; someone suffering from the effects of a heavy night on the mirrored tiles.

....

Usage:

'Your bird looks muntered' – I've just been to look at your budgie and it appears to be wasted on crack.

'They're a right munter' – when referring to a person at the bar who resembles a bag of intestines.

'I'm surrounded by munters' – shout it loud in the shopping centre and see what happens!

"Pearl Necklace"

Definition:

String of pearls worn around the stiff necks of rich hoity-toity ladies; the visual effect of a string of pearls worn around the neck after a man has shot his load all over it.

....

Usage:

'Darling, I want a pearl necklace' –
a perfectly acceptable thing to say while standing outside a jeweller's.

'Darling, I want a pearl necklace' – a perfectly acceptable thing to say on a date.

'Is that a pearl necklace?' – let's hope it is or that you inadvertently spilt correction fluid on yourself.

PISS

Definition:

Weak alcohol that looks and tastes the same
when it enters the body as when it leaves;
unexplained discolouration on a person's trousers
on Sunday mornings.

....

Usage:

'This wine tastes of piss' – useful phrase for a
restaurant critic.

'Are you taking the piss?' – could you please take
my drink away, bartender.

'It's not piss on my trousers. It's wine' –
useful excuse for a restaurant critic on a
Sunday morning.

PRICK TEASE

Definition:

A sexually attractive woman who charms the pants off a man but does not deliver, causing the man to feel frustrated and probably brag to his mates that he shagged her anyway.

....

Usage:

'You're a prick tease' – we both know that you're out of my league.

'She's a prick tease' – a man in response to his mates after a not-so-hot date.

'She's a prick tease' – don't ever say this about your girlfriend within her earshot, or you will no longer have a prick to tease.

"Pussy"

Definition:

Favourite porn term for a lady's front bottom; affectionate term for a pet cat.

....

Usage:

'My pussy loves the taste of fish' – when you're making polite conversation with the fishmonger.

'Can you feel my pussy in there?' – when you're at the vet's and your cat is cowering in its travel box.

'My pussy likes to be tickled' – when you're in bed with your partner (and your cat, of course).

QUIM

Definition:

The heavily guarded entrance to a lady's love tunnel; protected Brazilian rainforest; minge.

....

Usage:

'Doctor, I think there's something living deep in my quim' – useful medical phrase.

'I'd like a quim trim, please' – useful phrase when visiting the hairdresser on the doctor's recommendation.

'If I give you a Brazilian wax on that quim it could undermine the El Niño weather system' – oh dear, you've left it too late.

RIM JOB

Definition:

To lick someone's anal cavity, also known as rimming; derogatory term akin to a kiss-arse or a brown-noser; the reconditioning of car wheels.

....

Usage:

'What does that rim job require?' – one should always be cautious when a mechanic says, 'You need a rim job.'

'That rim job you did was great!' – to a mechanic, regarding the improvements he has made to your car's wheels.

'I'd love another rim job' – to a mechanic when asking for anilingus.

RING-PIECE

Definition:

A common term for an annoying twat;
another name for anus.

....

Usage:

*'After that curry last night, my ring-piece is singing
like Vera Lynn on speed!'* – thank yourself for
remembering to put a roll of toilet paper in the
fridge before you went to bed.

'What a ring-piece!' – what an idiot/twat/tool;
make sure that you can make a swift exit if you're
saying this about someone who is bigger than you.

'What a ring-piece!' – say this to your friend when
she shows you her engagement ring.

RUG MUNCHER

Definition:

A tuppence licker; a muff diver; a very hungry person in a rug shop.

....

Usage:

'Oi, let go, you rug munchers!' – exclamation of an angry shop assistant on seeing a small colony of rats feeding on the stock of fine Persian rugs.

'They look like a rug muncher' – useful descriptive phrase when you see someone with wool threads hanging from the corners of their mouth.

'Get me the head rug muncher!' – probably the least useful phrase in the English language.

"Schlong"

Definition:

A man's penis of decent size for slapping against his own thighs; originates from the German word *schlange* meaning 'snake'; used to describe something as being masculine or powerful; a moron.

....

Usage:

'That's one mighty schlong you have there' – that's a very impressive snake you have there.

'That's one mighty schlong you have there' – that's the biggest penis I've ever seen.

'Thatsch a mighty schlong way from here' – Sean Connery visiting your neck of the woods and complaining about the distance he will have to travel for a pint at your local pub.

SHAG

Definition:

A brand of pouch tobacco; a stupidly named dance;
a type of fluffy carpet; the act of fornication.

....

Usage:

'Fancy a shag?' – chat-up line involving the
proffering of one's pouch and a lighter.

'Fancy a deep shag?' – used by carpet sales
assistants to determine a customer's
sexual preferences.

'I really enjoyed that shag' – said by someone with
a roll-up in their mouth after a dance on a fluffy
carpet followed by a damn good rogering.

SHIT

Definition:

That which is excreted from the mouth of a liar; that which is excreted from the arse; a word to describe someone's performance in bed where the other person is left feeling like they've only had a rehearsal; that which a rabbit considers to be a wholesome meal.

....

Usage:

'You're shit in the sack' – well, let's try it on a bed like everyone else.

'Yuck! Is that shit on your fingers?' – stop licking them then.

'You talk a lot of shit' – I have to because I sell manure for a living.

SPOOGE

Definition:

A term used to describe cum; the act of a man shooting his load; to be excited by something; unexplained smear marks on computer screens.

....

Usage:

'There's spooge all over the carpet' – this carpet needs more than a vacuum to remove those dried-on stains.

'What's this spooge mark on my screen?' – likely to be said after a colleague has been working on your machine and has found your holiday snaps.

'Whenever I go there, I end up covered in spooge!' – what to say when complaining to your partner about the state of the shed.

SPUNK

Definition:

Australian term for a good-looking boy; American term for bravery; British term for sex wee.

....

Usage:

'Look at that spunky spunk!' – Australian girl on seeing a British boy after he has played pocket billiards without a tissue.

'He's full of spunk' – American girl on seeing a brave boy with nuts ready to burst.

'How come I always end up in the spunk?' – the obvious response when a Brit finds themselves lying in the wet patch.

"Strumpet"

Definition:

A person who loses their pants on a regular basis, usually on someone else's bedroom floor; a misspelling of trumpets.

....

Usage:

'I love the strumpet at Christmas time' – often heard when there's a brass band playing.

'I love the strumpet at Christmas time' – often heard at Christmas parties throughout the land.

'You ain't nothing but a strumpet!' – shouted by an angry parent when they hear their teen creep into the house at four in the morning with a trumpet under their arm.

TEA-BAGGING

Definition:

The dipping of a man's gonads into another person's mouth, imitating the act of brewing tea.

....

Usage:

'Fancy a bit of teabagging?' – something your granny asks you when your tea looks a bit weak.

'Fancy a bit of teabagging?' – if someone says this to you, just say no.

'I got teabagged last night' – if your colleague says this to you, just smile politely and hand them a bottle of mouthwash.

TITS

Definition:

A variety of bird found in the garden (in the jaws of the cat); people who wear bow ties; people who get excited about art (except art with tits in it); the contents of the top half of a bikini.

....

Usage:

'Tits out for the lads!' – phrase used by male ornithologists keen to see some tits.

'It's all gone tits up' – when a woman slips on a banana skin.

'Stop making a tit of yourself' – take that bow tie off.

TOOL

Definition:

Versatile word that describes any annoying person who is a bit slow on the uptake; someone who thinks they're the dog's danglies; a man's dangler; a try-hard; a workman's equipment.

....

Usage:

'You're a complete tool' – go back to the cave from which you crawled out of.

'That's a big tool!' – to be said when the plumber comes round with a very large wrench.

'That's a really big tool!' – when the plumber drops his trousers.

TOSSER

Definition:

One who throws cabers, wellies and other pointless things; a proponent of solo hand sports; a square with no sense of humour.

....

Usage:

'I am a tosser' – proud boast of an Olympic wellie thrower in relation to his work.

'I am a tosser' – proud boast of an Olympic wellie thrower in relation to his sex life.

'Don't be such a tosser' – OK, you've had a childish laugh in the staff room with the other teachers, now give this book back to the kid you confiscated it from.

"Twat"

Definition:

Someone who gets an erection just from listening to Mozart; a woman's front bottom.

....

Usage:

'What a twat!' – appropriate thing to say to someone who trips over.

'Were you always an arsehole and a twat, or were you once just a twat?' – appropriate thing to say to someone who puts sombre songs on the jukebox.

'What a twat!' – appropriate thing to say when presented with a bush that is in urgent need of topiary.

Definition:

Someone with a better-looking partner than you; anyone who wins the lottery; a penis.

....

Usage:

'They're a right wang!' – a lottery winner who makes a valid point.

'Complete and utter wang' – someone who wins the lottery twice.

'A bit of a wang' – a person who cheats on their partner and wins a quid on the lottery.

WANKER

Definition:

Anyone who drives a better car than you;
someone who likes to indulge in a handjob.

....

Usage:

'You wanker!' – your actions indicate to me that
you enjoy spanking the monkey.

'You wanker!' – in response to noticing that a
person's arm is more developed than their
other arm.

'Look at that rich wanker' – you have an automatic
right to abuse someone who works hard for their
money while you sit on your arse reading a
book of rude words.

"Wazzer"

Definition:

A bit of an idiot; someone who hogs the dance floor; a jobsworth; an urgent need to use the facilities.

....

Usage:

'Go and tell that wazzer over there' – a couldn't-care-less response when you're contesting that someone has taken your parking space.

'I could do with a wazzer' – useful when caught short during an interview.

'I could do without the wazzer' – when referring to someone who is cramping your style.

SWEARY
SYNONYMS

TOP WORDS FOR A MAN'S PENIS

Crotch rocket

Dick

John Thomas

Love truncheon

Meat missile

Nob

Pink oboe

Pork sword

Willy

TOP WORDS FOR A LADY'S FRONT BOTTOM

Bacon sandwich

Brazilian rainforest

Clunge

Fur burger

Gash

Hair pie

Minge

Muff

Quim

Snatch

Twat

TOP WORDS FOR AN
ARSEHOLE

Back alley

Brown eye

Bum crack

Chocolate starfish

Dirt box

Dumper

Fudge department

Hershey highway

Marmite machine

Poop chute

Sphincter

TOP WORDS FOR FEMALE WANKING

Bean-flicking

Beef-curtain-pulling

Brushing the beaver

Clit-hopping

Fanny-scratching

Muff-buffing

Petting the kitty

Playing the clitar

Polishing the pearl

TOP WORDS FOR
MALE WANKING

Choking the chicken

Five-finger shuffle

Jerking off

Making your third eye cry

Merchant bank

Rifle practice

Spanking the monkey

Switching to manual

Tommy tank

Three shakes more than a piss

Trouser snooker

TOP WORDS FOR
BREASTS

Airbags

Babylons

Bazookas

Bristols

Gazongas

Hooters

Jugs

Knockers

Melons

Norks

Tatas

Udders

TOP WORDS FOR BALLS

Bollocks

Cajones

Family jewels

Gonads

Goolies

Knackers

Nuts

Plums

Stones

Teabags

TOP WORDS FOR DIARRHOEA

Back-door trots

Botty sick

Dookie drawers

Fudge fountain

Green-apple quickstep

Ploppy bottom

Pudding hammock

Runs

Shits

Squits

TOP WORDS FOR
CUM

Baby batter

Cock chowder

Dick spit

Gentleman's relish

Jerk sauce

Jizz

Love juice

Man gravy

Satan's eggnog

Sex wee

Spooge

TOP WORDS FOR
DILDO

Cock on call

Girl's best friend

Meat substitute

Mother's little helper

Phallic friend

Plastic pal

TOP WORDS FOR
BALL-SUCKING

Ball-bathing

Eating your veg

Gob-stopping

Nut-munching

Sack-sampling

Swilling the spheres

Tea-bagging

Twins' day out

TOP WORDS FOR A
LARGE PENIS

Beef bayonet

Captain cock

Chopper

Donkey dick

Man cannon

Pant python

Schlong

Third leg

Wang

TOP WORDS FOR
EJACULATING

Blast off

Blow your load

Bust a nut

Cream your jeans

Pop your cork

Spill your seed

Spread your man mustard

TOP WORDS FOR ERECTIONS

Boner

Hard-on

His manliness

Horn

Pitching a tent

Rod of steel

Stiffy

Throbber

Woody

TOP WORDS FOR
PISSED

Battered

Bladdered

Rat-arsed

Shit-faced

Smashed

Twatted

Wankered

TOP WORDS FOR
FUCKING

Banging

Buttering the bread

Dancing the horizontal tango

Dipping your wick

Filling the cream doughnut

Laying the pipe

Shagging

TOP WORDS FOR
ORGY

Communal fuckathon

Crowded house

Fruit bowl

One big hug

Snakes and fannies

Spaghetti junction

If you're interested in finding out more about our books, find us on Facebook at **Summersdale Publishers** and follow us on Twitter at **@Summersdale**.

www.summersdale.com